Building a Legacy: The Family-First
Entrepreneur's Guide to Financial
Freedom"

I0409149

INTRODUCTION

It is extremely challenging to consider yourself a monetarily free individual when you are as yet taking care of obligation, yet it is something that you can do. The best way to set goals and achieve financial independence is through the use of a budget.

Every month, your profits and losses will be shown in a budget. Additionally, it will assist you in determining the amount of debt you have and the amount of money you must save to reduce it (or at least make it manageable). Whenever you've accomplished that, there are different procedures to set aside more cash. This advice will direct you on the path to financial independence, whether you want to change jobs, reduce your spending, avoid common investment blunders, or cut back on spending.

• Keep a spending log.

The best way to see where your money is going is to keep track of it. A notebook, an app for budgeting, or a pen and paper are all options. Try these suggestions if you want to stick with just one strategy that suits you best:

• Make use of a variety of tools, such as a budgeting spreadsheet and smartphone app.

Screen your spending for quite some time from the get go, then broaden it out north of a year (or longer).

• By honing your skills, you can raise your revenue.

Develop your talents so you can work for the top companies in your industry. If you're looking for a better job in your field but lack experience, you can start off as an apprentice or enroll in training programs that will teach you the necessary skills (and maybe even be kind in advance!). Additionally, you can use these skills as side jobs to increase your income.

• Always pay off your debts. The best way to get out of debt is to pay it off. It's not always easy, but with a little determination and work, you can do it.

• Lower your expenses.

To avoid eating out, make your own food at home. You can also buy things when they are on sale or cheap. Also, make sure you don't buy things you don't need.

•Draft out a spending plan you can stick to.

The first step toward financial freedom is to establish a budget. You genuinely should make one that works for yourself and not simply something you are told to follow. Although it doesn't have to be difficult or complicated, making a budget does require some preparation.

• You will need to know how much money you make each month and how much goes toward bills like rent or utilities. Create an expense sheet with distinct categories (such as food) based on those numbers. When this accounting sheet has been made, it becomes more straightforward in light of the fact that every one of your costs are held inside every classification, so there's no mystery included while attempting to sort out where precisely your Naira went!

By developing smart habits, you can achieve financial independence. Money is only one component of financial freedom. It's about being able to do whatever you want, be who you want, and spend your time doing whatever you want.

Without having to worry about how much money is still in your bank account, you can lead a life that is tailored to your requirements and objectives when you are financially independent. There are no shortcuts to financial independence; however, the aforementioned advice can get you started.

CHAPTER 1
UNDERSTANDING FINANCIAL FREEDOM

The majority of people want to achieve financial independence. Usually, being financially free means having enough money saved, invested, and on hand to live the life we want for ourselves and our families. It means increasing our savings so that we can retire or pursue the career we want without being compelled to make a predetermined annual salary. Independence from the rat race implies that our money works for us rather than the other way around.

How do you free yourself from debt? You must eliminate your consumer debts, establish a safety net of savings, and generate sufficient passive income through investing or business ownership to cover your current and anticipated future living expenses in order to achieve financial independence.

We are hindered from achieving our most important financial goals by our mounting debt, financial emergencies, excessive consumer spending, and other issues. These difficulties affect everyone, but the twelve habits listed below can help you get your finances in order.

• Establish financial and lifestyle goals, both large and small; make a strategy for achieving those goals.

• Set aside sufficient funds to meet all of your requirements; adhere to this program; make sure you pay off all of your credit cards in full so you don't owe as much money and keep an eye on your credit.

• Start investing and working with a financial advisor; keep up with the latest tax laws; foster mechanized commitments through your organization's retirement plan; make a fund for an emergency.

• Reduce your spending; whenever you can, be thrifty; and do not be afraid to negotiate for better offers or to ask for them.

• Take care of your personal belongings because repairs are less expensive than replacements; however, more strikingly, deal with yourself and stay solid.

Financial freedom means that you have enough money to cover your living costs and pay for many of your life's goals without having to work or spend any time or effort working to make money. One or both of the following might be included in these resources:

•Independent Income An independent income is earned through a business, government benefits, or other regular income sources that do not require you to work (in exchange for money). Assuming you qualify, government managed retirement benefits show up each month. You can receive payments regardless of how much time you put into your business if you have developed it to the point where you are able to delegate day-to-day management responsibilities. In the event that you own an investment property, you get a lease installment one time per month, in spite of the fact that property the executives frequently requires property support and risks leasing to a one or more occupant installments).

You are financially independent if you have a sufficient independent income to cover your needs and living expenses.

• Abundant Assets Assets that support financial freedom typically consist of cash in bank accounts, property of value, and investments in securities. You must first invest, usually a lot of money over a long time, in an asset before you can use it to achieve financial freedom. For instance, the majority of financial planners will advise you that regularly contributing to a 401(K) is essential for your long-term financial security and stability. If people start investing early (in their 20s, 30s, or even 40s), this may be the case for many people. But if you wait until you're 50 or older to start investing, you won't have enough time to benefit from the power of compound interest. When inflation is taken into account, their contributions will rarely even double.

Using assets to achieve financial independence may result in issues. Consider it a balancing act. Utilizing this strategy to pay for your everyday costs and needs, you really want to offer a resource for have sufficient money for your bills. Problems can arise if you can't sell an asset, like real estate, quickly enough to have the money available before your bill is due. Such individuals might be referred to as "cash-poor millionaires." Their resources may be esteemed at more than $1M, yet they can't get to that worth quickly enough to utilize. When you don't have enough assets to turn into cash before you die, you run the risk of running into a bigger problem. Fundamentally, assuming you go through the entirety of your resources excessively quick, you will be left with nothing to take care of for your bills.

The majority of financially stable households employ a combination of these two strategies. They might get their own income from social security, from a business, or from dividend-paying securities they've invested in. However, they probably also have enough assets in the stock market and the housing market to give them financial security, knowing they can always rely on them.

Life Objectives

Write down how much cash (resources and pay) you really want to pay for the way of life you need. Include the year in which you want to accomplish your objectives and whether or not you will need to pay for them. The more specific your goals are, the more likely it is that you will achieve them. The next step is to look backward to your current age and set regular financial milestones. These could be specific amounts saved or assets acquired.

•Budget Keeping

A monthly household spending plan is essential for ensuring that all bills are paid and that investments and the creation of an independent income are on track. Instead of allowing yourself to succumb to the urge to spend extravagantly, regularly establishing a budget clarifies your goals and strengthens your willpower. Your ability to build wealth is at risk when you use credit cards and high-interest consumer loans. You can review the five fundamental guidelines that you should adhere to for additional guidance on how to budget.

•Put in Your Time and Obligations

Understudy loans, contracts, and comparative credits ordinarily have a much lower pace of interest than Visas and retail location cards, making them less risky to your funds. With charge cards, you could wind up accumulating large number of dollars of exorbitant premium obligations. Suffocating in the red for a really long time is the direct inverse of freedom. Since debt implies a duty and even servitude, which obviously contradicts the idea of financial freedom.

• Save yourself money first

That is a standard suggestion from monetary specialists. Take advantage of your employer's retirement plan's matching contributions to the fullest. It is moreover a phenomenal plan to have a mechanized store from your manager into a backup stash (or a robotized move from your making sure) that can be tapped for unforeseen consumptions. For an Individual Retirement Account, you might also want to think about setting up an automated contribution to a brokerage.Nevertheless, keep in mind that the amount that should be saved is a subject of intense debate, and the suitability of such a fund may even be in question in some instances.

•Contribute

There is not a lot better, and not any more time tested method for developing your money than through effective financial planning. Whether you choose an IRA or a 401(k), now is the time to conduct research and select a starting point. However, begin! The most significant step is ththat

•Monitor your credit report

A person's credit report affects the interest rates on credit cards, store cards, and loans for cars, trucks, homes, or refinances. Additionally, it

has an effect on unrelated things like the premiums for life and auto insurance. The argument goes that a person who is careless with their finances may also be careless in other areas of life, like driving and drinking. The fact of the matter is that, as a group, people with lower credit scores are more likely to get into accidents and to file more claims with their insurance companies than people with higher credit scores. In the same way that a man who is 23 years old and is not married is not a bad driver, this does not mean that someone with poor credit is a bad driver. Be that as it may, he will pay higher month to month expenses since
he is youthful, single, and male. Unfortunate credit is only one of many gamble pools insurance agency use while deciding your month to month expense.

•Bonus

Many Americans are afraid that negotiating prices for goods and services will make them appear more expensive. Many people from other nations would advise Americans to overcome this cultural disadvantage. You could be able to save thousands of dollars annually. Particularly, smaller businesses are usually willing to negotiate. Discounts may be available when you make multiple purchases or in bulk.

• Learn What Must Be Learned
 Keep up with stock exchange financial news and events, and don't be afraid to change your financial investment portfolio. Information is the absolute best guard against the

individuals who mislead unsophisticated purchasers to turn a fast buck. Regarding your credit card, you should be aware of your credit limit to avoid overspending. It is your duty to remain aware of these particulars.

• Take Care of Your Things

By taking good care of your home and your belongings, you can extend the life of everything from lawn mowers and automobiles to shoes and clothing. Imagine not having to buy shoes and clothes as frequently as you do. You could keep your car for longer and save money in the process. Saving money requires regular maintenance.

• Live within your means:

Mastering a frugal lifestyle by thinking about how to live life to the fullest with as little as possible is not as difficult as it may appear. A lot of wealthy people spent less money than they earned. Frugality is not an impediment to living a minimalist lifestyle or a call to extreme hoarding or dumpster diving. Frugality is buying important things at the right price and taking good care of them.

•Get Master Exhortation

Regardless of whether you are not yet where you have started storing up abundance, getting master monetary exhortation to instruct yourself and assist with using sound judgment will assist you with forestalling issues. Numerous reputable professionals are available to assist you at no cost or for minimal fees, including accredited financial counselors, nonprofit credit counseling agencies, and your local county extension specialist.

• Maintain a Healthy Body and Mind Insurance premiums skyrocket as a result of illnesses and obesity, and poor health may necessitate earlier retirement with lower monthly benefits. While taking care of your health won't solve all of your money problems, it will help you form habits that will get you closer to financial independence. How Will I Know When I Have Reached Financial Independence? When you have enough income streams or assets to cover your basic living expenses and any additional discretionary spending you desire without relying on a traditional job or career, you will have achieved financial freedom. As a result, you can travel, pursue your interests and passions, work or not, and live life how you want.

A comprehensive budget that includes all of your expenses, including housing, food, utilities, transportation, insurance, and discretionary spending, will help you determine whether you have achieved financial freedom.

Then, at that point, you'll need to think about your pay from all sources, like ventures, rental pay, and any seasonal work, to your costs. If your income is higher than your expenses, you may be on your way to financial independence.

It is essential to keep in mind that achieving financial independence is not a destination but rather a journey, and achieving your objectives may necessitate time and effort. But you can live the life you've always wanted to live with careful planning, disciplined saving and investing, and a willingness to make short-term sacrifices.

Keep in mind that achieving financial independence requires taking small steps in the right direction. Keep up the excellent work and don't let setbacks discourage you. You can achieve this!

CHAPTER 2
BALANCING FAMILY AND BUSINESS

Managing a family and a business at the same time is a difficult task that entrepreneurs face every day. Family and business are two of life's most important aspects. Trying to strike a balance between the two often feels overwhelming because they both require a lot of individual attention and dedication.

Throughout everyday life, there will never be a manual on the most proficient method to be working guardians and make things work. Your sole purpose as an entrepreneur is to explore new opportunities, develop effective strategies, and achieve results. You do this for personal growth, portfolio extension, and monetary improvement.

However, when your family is involved, things can get a little more complicated. Because you are now responsible for not only yourself but also your family, your work rate and results must improve. It can be difficult to maintain a healthy balance between your new responsibilities and the attention you used to devote solely to your business.

The following guidelines will help you in finding that all-important balance between the two, whether you are just starting your entrepreneurial journey and are considering starting a family of your own in the long run or are currently rooted in the trenches of both.

• Make a Daily practice

As full-time or seasonal working guardians will be aware, getting to know each other with the family is fundamental. It's not uncommon for us to become frustrated and stressed out when our precious time is wasted. As a result, being mindful of how you spend your time is crucial for working parents. Implement a daily routine that works for you and your loved ones to give your day some structure.

A routine not only keeps you productive and organized, but it also makes your days more predictable, which saves you time and energy. Because things won't always go according to plan, set aside a certain amount of time for each task, both personal and professional, and be willing to be flexible.

Instances of accommodating schedules you can begin executing today:

• Make a list of things to do each night for the next day.
• Decide when you will check and respond to emails throughout the day, such as once at 9 a.m. and once at 6 p.m.
• Begin meal preparation.
• Make Meals a Priority

For a family, mealtimes are the most sacred time. It's during these valuable pockets of time that you get to bond, get up to speed, and develop that culture of harmony. It has been demonstrated that families who eat together are happier and healthier. Other advantages include enhanced family dynamics, increased stability within the home, and improved behavior and literacy. In addition, as a parent, you can learn something new about your child or spouse that day, which aids in reconnection, bonding, and improved relationships. Are you new to family meals? In the beginning, allot one evening per week to family dinners, and gradually increase that number as time goes on. Additionally, try to involve everyone in the cooking process. Not exclusively will this assist them with building another expertise and find out about nourishment, but at the same time it's an extraordinary method for interfacing and will assist with creating deep rooted good dieting propensities.

• Set Specific Goals and Maintain Discipline

While it may be simple to outline your business objectives, have you considered combining them with your family objectives? It's good business sense to have clear long-term plans and goals, but it's even more important to keep your family's best interests in mind. Have a precise (and attainable!) goal each day. set a goal for your family and business, and work toward achieving it. As you develop as a family and a business, the goals will assist you in achieving milestones. In the end, your family goal should include more than just what you should do for them. It should also include what you should do together. Your family's psychological and emotional needs should be one of your daily objectives, even though money comes and goes. Therefore, when you do have spare time, spend it with your family.

• Accept Self-Care

Most of the time, you'll feel worn out. It demonstrates a great deal of devotion to your family to give it your all, but the question remains: Who will look after you? You might be the glue that holds everything together, but overworking the glue makes it break and become weaker. Poor performance as a parent and as a manager could result from neglecting your own mental and physical health.

It's critical to carve out opportunity to re-energize and satisfy your own necessities. When you disconnect from the things in your life that cause you stress, you'll be able to reenergize and refresh your mindset, giving you more ideas, willpower, and creativity to face life head-on.

With discipline, an open attitude, and assurance, it's feasible to adjust both work and family effectively and have everything pan out in support of yourself.

CHAPTER 3
IDENTIFYING YOUR PRIORITIES

Simply making a decision is essential to maintaining a business. It will be easier to choose the best option if you keep the most important things in mind. As an entrepreneur, you'll have to deal with a lot of problems and wear many hats. Tasks and priorities for each day are likely to be mixed up and alter when new emergencies and developments occur. You will need to quickly adjust to these low-level changes if you want to succeed, but you will also need to have a strong "higher perspective" reasoning that serves as a foundation for your day-to-day decisions. Without serious adherence to your most critical, certain level requirements, your entire strategy gambles with falling to pieces. Your entrepreneurial operations should be built on these five "golden" priorities, which should come before any other high- or low-level factors:

• New ideas.

During the ideation and brainstorming phase, innovation is usually the first thing that comes to mind when you think about starting your own business. Throughout the entirety of your business development, you must keep this in mind; You won't be able to stand out from competitors if you don't innovate. Innovation does not necessitate coming up with a brand-new concept; It could involve bringing an older model up to date for a new environment or bringing together two previously distinct concepts.

It is up to you to innovate, but innovation must take precedence over convenience. In the event that given the decision between leaving what makes you special or continuing onward with more serious gamble, face the more prominent challenge. You will always come back to haunt you if you lose your uniqueness in the field.

•Profitability.

Nothing bad can be said about the way that a ton of business people start their professions considering money related objectives. However, some people prioritize expansion over profitability. They might prioritize growth over sustainability by investing all of their earnings in the acquisition of new equipment or the recruitment of new staff members. This bet has the potential to pay off at times, but overall, it is a very bad choice. Profitability is still important, even if you started a business for no money; You won't be able to grow the business, support yourself, or invest in your own future if you don't make money. Deciding to assume a misfortune in the present moment may periodically be a vital penance, however in a more extensive viewpoint, your emphasis on productivity can never be deserted to succeed.

• Cash flow

Your company's cash flow should be your top financial priority. Simply put, cash flow is a look at how much money you have now and how that money will change soon. For instance, you might have $1,500 in the bank but anticipate receiving payment for an invoice of $3,000 and are aware that a bill of $1,600 is coming up. To ensure that all of your bills are paid on time, it is essential to manage your cash on hand. Since your business is beneficial doesn't mean you're free. Even though they appeared to be profitable on paper, there have been businesses that have run out of cash and closed shop.

By assigning at least one person to actively monitor your cash flow, you can tightly manage it. Before making major financial decisions, carefully consider your cash on hand and implement procedural stopgaps to maintain cash flow. To avoid non-payment issues, you can, for instance, postpone bill payments until the very last day possible and conduct credit checks on your customers.

•Culture.

Your company's culture is what will keep your team working hard. Even if your culture is in favor of promising new opportunities, if it starts to deteriorate, you run the risk of alienating your core workforce and having a demoralized core team to propel your business forward.

Let's say you get a new customer and are worried about how to handle the work. Initiating a progression of social changes, for example, stricter planning rules and more regulatory cycles, could cause more damage to your organization's resolve than great for your organization's proficiency. Think carefully about how your actions will affect the culture.

• Improvement.

Last but not least, one of your top priorities should be getting better. You will need to put in a lot of effort to gradually adapt your business to the new circumstances because markets, customers, and businesses never stay the same for very long. You will learn to continuously and significantly improve your products, services, infrastructure, processes, branding, and marketing as you gain entrepreneurial experience. On a landscape that is changing, only the adaptable survive.

Never let something less important get in the way of one of these priorities. Regardless of the circumstances, the most successful entrepreneurs of our time have maintained these priorities consistently. You won't have any trouble paving your own path to the top if you are able to do that while also managing the chaos of day-to-day management.

CHAPTER 4
CREATING A FAMILY-CENTERED BUSINESS

A family business is typically run by a partner, a sibling, or other close family members, but it can also be run by a best friend. The company's members combine their skills and knowledge to either provide a service that the community lacks or enhance existing offerings.

Advantages of Family Businesses

Family businesses offer a plethora of benefits, which are what make them so appealing.

• You Know Your Employees Already

Onboarding a new employee always takes time because you need to learn about their personality and working style. It's a lot simpler when you recruit relatives, as you definitely know them and how they impart. You'll even be aware of behaviors that could be problematic and be able to address them.

Additionally, there is no need for an interview when hiring family members. This is consistently a tedious piece of beginning a business, particularly when you really want to run individual verifications and affirm the legitimacy of certificates.

•Agreeable Air

Definitely realizing everybody likewise makes an incredible work climate. For example, you're ready to have legitimate discussions instead of simply casual conversation.

• An Advantage Over Other Businesses: Working for a family business means you'll have a close-knit team of employees who are all more committed to the company's success than if they worked for any employer.

• Greater adaptability Family members are also more likely to be understanding when a family member has additional responsibilities and needs to change their work hours or take time off. Given that everybody is focused on the outcome of the business, it's not difficult to be adaptable

• Clients Favor Privately-owned companies

Clients like knowing that there's a family in the background. The brand picture is one of trust, difficult work, and fellowship. This is particularly obvious when you likewise treat your clients as family.

Disadvantages of Family Businesses

Family businesses naturally come with a number of drawbacks as well. Before deciding whether or not a family business is the best option for you, it is essential that you evaluate these drawbacks.

You can't run a family business and expect relationships to stay the same.

• Family relationships will change. It can be easy to create conflicts that last a lifetime, so the challenge is to ensure that changes are beneficial. One trouble specifically is the way that one of you should be in control. It is essential to keep in mind that management does not extend to family life.

•Your Children Ought to In any case Work Somewhere else

Though it very well might be enticing to give your children a task at your business straight out of secondary everyday schedule, this isn't recommendable. They will learn a lot more about how other businesses operate and broaden their global experience by working for other businesses in the beginning. The disadvantage is that rather than joining your company, your children may choose to work elsewhere permanently.

• Promotions Must Be Based on Merit Members of a family may anticipate receiving a promotion for their family status rather than their role in the business. Promoting employees based on merit is essential to the success of your company. Employees outside of the family will also have equal opportunities as a result of this.

• Creativity Can Be Stifled Sometimes the atmosphere of a family business can easily become overly casual. Because of this and the fact that you all come from similar backgrounds, innovation may be limited.

How to Start a Family Business?

Just like with any other kind of business, starting a family business requires a plan. Participate in this planning with everyone who will be employed at the company to ensure that you are all on the same page.

Step 1: Define Your Business Idea

Everyone should be enthusiastic about the idea. If you want to make a living from your business, you should just work a regular 9-to-5 job if you want to. Find an idea that brings together everyone's interests and goals in life.

Step 2: Determine Each Family Member's Role

Each family member must have a distinct role with established responsibilities. Pick the jobs as per abilities and foundation as well as shortcomings. A positional hierarchy can help reduce conflict by ensuring that everyone knows who to report to.

Step 3: Set Out Rules for Maintaining the Business

It very well may be challenging to make the progress from relatives to colleagues. Providing clear guidelines will be extremely helpful.

First and foremost, you must ensure that everyone separates family concerns from business matters. For instance, a more youthful relative might end up having superb initiative abilities and be an extraordinary decision for a director. Resentment can be avoided by keeping personal relationships out of business.

Additionally, make sure to set aside time for family time and refrain from discussing business at these times. After all, you want people who didn't join the business to still feel like they were always a part of the family.

Step 4: Discuss Risk

The process of starting a business is always risky. There is a possibility that your business will fail, resulting in the loss of your investment. Make sure that all of the family members who want to invest in the business are willing to take the risk by discussing this with them.

Step 5: Choose Workloads

At first, working for a family business will be much more difficult than working for an established company. You will have to put the business ahead of many other obligations, work long hours, and spend less time with partners or children who are not involved in the business. All of this will require a lower income than you are likely accustomed to. This needs to be made clear to family members, and they need to be willing to make the necessary sacrifices.

Step 6: Discuss Ownership and Compensation

You will need to settle on a starting salary for each employee. You might pay a compensation, utilize time-based compensations, or give relatives a specific portion of the benefits.Even using them simultaneously is possible.

Regardless, you must ensure that your choice complies with state wage laws.

You must agree on the percentage of the business each family member owns, if any, in addition to the payment. This will include the share they get if you sell the company. When deciding the future course of your company, voting rights will also be determined.

Step 7: Set out Open doors for Development

Very much like while working for some other organization, colleagues will need to get the opportunity to fill in their professions. Talk to each person individually to learn about their objectives and how your company can provide the best opportunities.

Step 8: Specify Plans for Succession and Exit

A family member may also decide to leave the business to pursue other interests. Particularly if the employee owns a stake in the business, you must specify what will happen in this scenario and how the employee will be compensated.

Additionally, the business's founders will eventually retire. Set out the terms of handing over the business from the beginning.

Step 9: Deal with the Lawful Side

When you have every one of the above subtleties resolved, it's vital to suitably structure your business. Contract a legal counselor to draw up the vital records and ask a business specialist for exhortation on perspectives like the strategy, representative advantages, retirement plans, and duties.

Step 10: Hire outside of the family

There is a good chance that you won't

be able to find all of the skills you need in just your family. Fill this information hole with outside enlists. It is essential to treat these workers as if they were members of your family, providing them with the same advancement opportunities and involving them to the same extent when marking milestones.

Family-owned businesses can be extremely profitable. Everybody at your organization will endeavor to give a valiant effort to ultimately benefit the family. They might even want to create a company or leave a legacy for future generations.

Be that as it may, you should cautiously explore extreme business choices to try not to make a crack in your loved ones. To see a positive outcome, you'll should be knowledgeable in how to begin a little privately-run company, have a strong strategy, and make anything strides are important to permit your organization to develop.

In point of fact, just knowing how to start a family business is only the beginning: You'll also need to be ready to tackle any challenges that come with running a family business. Learn how to deal with issues before they arise by reading our blog post on three common issues that affect family businesses.

CHAPTER 5
FINANCIAL PLANNING

The majority of people are interested in better managing their personal finances and have heard about the advantages of personal financial planning. But sometimes it can seem so overwhelming. In the event that you don't know where to begin, this monetary arranging groundwork can help. It lays out eight easy steps to take control of your finances and establishes priorities for anyone at any stage of their financial life.

Step 1. Create a financial plan and look over it.

This is a fundamental written list of objectives, methods, and timetables for achieving these objectives: paying off debts, buying your first home, funding or managing a retirement fund, supporting your children's education, etc.This strategy will motivate you to assume responsibility for completing your task list, whether you write it down on a yellow pad, in a spreadsheet, or with the assistance of a certified financial planner (CFP) professional. It gives you direction, gives you a standard against which to measure your progress, and helps you prioritize how best to spend your money.

Changes in marital status, job loss, retirement, the birth of a child, or a family member's death should all be taken into account when revising your plan on a regular basis.

Step 2. Sort through your financial documents.

It's a lot simpler to effectively deal with your funds on the off chance that you understand what those funds are. Therefore, gather the following financial documents:

Documents related to your investment accounts, tax returns, mortgages, credit cards, insurance policies, and estate planning should be organized so that you can quickly locate and access them. You will be able to set the stage for your future goals and priorities by gathering them all together. This will make it easier for you to assess where you are at right now. And keeping in mind that you're busy, remember to stock your own belongings. This not only provides a record for your insurance company in the event that your possessions are lost due to a theft or natural disaster, but it also documents their value for planning purposes.

Step 3. Determine your total wealth. Calculate your net worth after organizing your financial records. Simply subtract what you owe from what you own to accomplish this. If your house, investments, bank accounts, and other assets are greater than your debts (mortgage, student loans, credit card debt, etc.), then you will have a positive net worth. Then again, on the off chance that you owe more than you own, you'll have a negative total assets.

Total assets is the best estimation of the condition of your monetary wellbeing and ought to be utilized as the reason for any monetary choices you make. Your annual net worth increase ought to be your objective. At year-end, you ought to recalculate your total assets and analyze it against last year's benchmark. You will immediately be able to see your progress if you do this.

Step 4. Organize your spending. The sources and destinations of your finances are detailed in a spending plan. Your salary, bonus, interest, and any other income you have are included in the inflows. Inflow is the part that is by and large least demanding to review. A comprehensive list of where your money goes is contained in the outflow section. The main surge ought to be your reserve funds. Your income will be equal to your expenditures if you live within your means.

No matter where you are in life or how much money you have, having a budget that keeps your spending in check should be a top priority for your finances. A spending plan distinguishes the key regions where you maintain that your assets should go and features squandered spending. Additionally, it may provide an early warning of upcoming financial issues. Consider utilizing a software package like Quicken or a spreadsheet to assist you if this is your first time making a spending plan. The amount of time and effort required to create your plan could be significantly reduced with the help of these tools.

Step 5. Fabricate a secret stash.

In a perfect world, you need to have sufficient money close by to cover three to a half year of fundamental everyday costs would it be a good idea for you lose your standard kinds of revenue. You may want to increase the number of months' worth of reserves depending on your job security. Self-employed people, for instance, may want to have reserves for a year, especially if their income is unpredictable.

Step 6. Reduce or eliminate debt for consumers.

Like a heavy anchor, debt impedes other financial endeavors. Reduce your consumer debt as soon as possible if credit cards, student loans, auto loans, and personal loans account for 15 to 20 percent or more of your monthly spending. Furthermore, why waste supports paying what are probably exceptionally exorbitant financing costs on your cards and credits?

Step 7. Create four important documents for estate planning.

Every adult ought to have a will: 2) a strong legal authority, which names somebody to deal with your legitimate and monetary undertakings in the event that you can't; (3) a living will, which specifies your preferences for life-sustaining medical care in the event of your incapacity; furthermore (4) a medical services strong legal authority, which designates somebody to manage your clinical advantages would it be a good idea for you at this point not have the option to. Various states have various names for the clinical archives, yet they're all basic to your shrewd monetary preparation.

Step 8. Get the right insurance.

Overseeing risk is vital for your drawn out monetary security. The purpose of insurance, including life, auto, and homeowner's policies, as well as medical and disability coverage, is to safeguard you from financial ruin. To put it another way, you buy insurance to cover costs you wouldn't be able to cover on your own. It's basic to remember that you ought to purchase protection when you don't require it, since when you really do require it, you can't get it.

CHAPTER 6
NURTURING RELATIONSHIP AND COMMUNICATION

In today's fast-paced society, it can be easy to forget that building a business relationship that benefits both parties is the true foundation of business success. Sadly, for those just starting out in business, it is frequently not a high priority. All in all, exactly how would you make and keep up with secure associations with your business contacts?

You can't totally distinguish between business relationships and your personal life: they both take time and effort to maintain. Read on for a few methods you can implement to improve your relationships in your business place.

•Carry out a framework

All connections require work, thus when you get going with the heap of different things expected of you consistently having a framework set up can help. Start by coming up with ideas and creating a map of all the points of contact between your company and the people you want to connect with, whether they are customers, prospects, clients, or just business connections. Try to make those interactions as individual as possible. Follow up with people who are making inquiries or orders to show them that you care and that they are appreciated.

• Communication is Key

Effective communication is essential. Listening to your business contacts and customers is the most effective way to demonstrate care and will also assist you in developing your system. For instance, is there an issue or issue that a many individuals are experiencing? Is there a way that you can fix that?

•Cause your contacts to feel extraordinary and significant

Exceed all expectations to make your contacts — whoever they might be — feel unique. You could say, woo them. For other business contacts and the individuals who could encourage your objectives or plan, be smart however not excessively full on or pushy. Send them all personalized birthday cards, for instance, to demonstrate your care; it's those kinds of individual contacts that put you aside. Try not to stress over the issue either, for there are sites you can visit online which make adding an individual touch to your gifts such a great deal simpler than it used to be.

You could send customers a birthday discount code or other personalized rewards to show that you value their business, or you could do something similar. Customers are individuals, and treating them as such will ensure repeat business, but some business owners fall into the trap of thinking of them as a faceless mob.

• Establish a trusting foundation

 For any business relationship, internal or external, to last, trust must be established. At the point when chiefs and representatives trust one another, the business runs all the more easily.

Customers are more likely to support a company if they have faith in it. To construct your business as a paragon of trust, you should work with uprightness, responsibility, and genuineness.

• Honor your contracts and agreements.

To avoid unwanted surprises, these collaborative efforts need to be laid out clearly and concisely. Be open and clear about roles and expectations. This demonstrates your company's sincerity and builds trust as a firm that sticks to its promises.

• Establish the relationship before making demands

You can't withdraw money from a bank account you haven't funded, and the same holds true for business relationships. You can anticipate receiving favors or assistance from people you haven't worked with before. You cannot put off getting what you need. By developing a rapport, you must first build the relationship.

While attempting to lay out a strong business relationship, it very well may be hard to tell where to start. As previously stated, honesty is essential here. The majority of business people view others as tools they can use to advance their own goals. Try to treat other people, whether they are customers, contacts from your business, or potential customers, as a means to an end. Soon, your relationships will flourish.

•Know your worth

While building any relationship, it is vital to comprehend and explain the worth that you propose to that relationship. Your worth isn't really restricted to your actual contributions. You must comprehend the other person's requirements and the ways in which your solutions can affect their lives, businesses, customers, and so forth. You need to know where you fit in the chain, what effect you have, and how you can help.

Emotions frequently take the lead in most of a person's most important relationships. It's rare for people to choose to hang out with people they don't like. Notwithstanding, in business, this isn't true; From a financial standpoint, it's all about demonstrating your worth and creating situations where everyone benefits. It is unlikely that the business relationship will last if you are unable to assist one another in increasing their income.

• Add a personal touch

Although it has been discussed numerous times throughout, this aspect is so crucial that it merits its own section. One of the best things you can do to ensure success is to treat each person your business interacts with individually. Consider how your brand reaches other people; The majority of people will do this via social media posts, comments, or emails. It can feel cold and unfriendly if these aren't personalized, so customize email templates and respond to inquiries as personally as you can.

Try to learn a little bit about the lives they lead outside of work about other business contacts to show that you care about them. After that, you can use what you've learned from them to develop rapport with them. Because you have demonstrated that you care, they are much more likely to listen to your ideas or proposals because they owe you the same courtesy.

CHAPTER 7
BUILDING A SUPPORTIVE NETWORK

In both their personal and professional lives, everyone requires a network of trustworthy contacts. These support networks can make the difference between feeling like you're on your own and being deeply connected to other entrepreneurs and having a team of friends, partners, or advisers to turn to when you're not sure where to go. This is especially true for entrepreneurs.

Seven suggestions for creating the ideal network to support your entrepreneurial objectives are provided here.

• Join a local social club.

 Joining a social club is a great way to expand your personal network, which is essential. Not exclusively will you be presented to incredible occasions, you'll likewise meet expected clients, representatives, and companions.Check out the Union League and Young Friends groups at the ballet, orchestra, and museums in your area for "Young Friends" memberships.

• Be a part of groups.

In the event that you're a female business person, investigate neighborhood sections of the Public Relationship of Ladies Entrepreneurs. Check out the local chapter of a national plumbers' association if you are thinking about starting a plumbing business. The sheer number of fields with associations will surprise you. Discounts on fantastic products, invitations to fantastic conferences, and a peer group are all possibilities. Since being an entrepreneur can be lonely, it's important to make friends. Naturally, there is also the Young Entrepreneur Council, of which I am a board member.

•Make a little gathering of five similar business people.

You might be familiar with these "mastermind" groups already. But what is a group of people who haven't mastered something yet? Whatever you want to call it, just build one quickly. Ensure that the four others you connect with don't have contending organizations, and consider ways you can help one another. I know of groups that meet every month and require each member to bring at least one lead for another group member to the meeting. Likewise, be aware of time. Because you are all entrepreneurs with a lot on your plate, limit your monthly time commitment to 60 to 90 minutes.

• Hold a monthly dinner or happy hour and invite new people.

Think about this your beginning up showcasing cost! Organize a gathering for a select group of people you want to meet. Make sure to personally meet and greet each person on your list and be strategic in your invitations. Permit every individual to bring a visitor on the off chance that it's a party time. Assuming you're facilitating a supper, it's alright to stretch out the greeting just to that individual. Also, make sure that your guests, not just you, will benefit from getting to know your other guests! I typically host dinner parties once a month because I enjoy cooking and hosting guests in my home. Right now in my vocation, my gatherings are more about spending time with my companions and common help. However, they're always fun! So don't make everything about business!

• Do not attempt to withdraw funds that have not been deposited.

It's truly out of line to email individuals requesting that they guide you when you don't bring anything to the table for them. Although it may sound harsh, it is true! Out of the hundreds of requests for mentoring I receive annually, the ones that ask, "Can I take you to coffee?" are the ones I typically respond to. The reason for this is that the person's small act demonstrates their belief in a relationship that benefits both parties. A good friend of mine started his entire business by taking people out for lunch, despite the fact that he barely had the money to do so. Additionally, he was successful in persuading a number of highly regarded individuals to join him for lunch and, ultimately, to provide funding for his company. In the event that you ask him his trick of the trade,

he'll let you know it was basically requesting that individual's lunch.
•Offer in return.
My work in philanthropy has resulted in the most significant professional connections for me. I frequently join the marketing committees of the non-profits with which I collaborate to meet new people and share ideas. They get a firsthand look at my abilities and evaluate me as a coworker. Because it will backfire, you shouldn't join an organization you don't care about just to meet new people. However, generating new business will be a pleasant outcome if you have the chance to collaborate with a worthy organization.
• Participate in panels and conferences.
Working, whether at home or in the office, is something I really enjoy. I also dislike being away from the office during the week, despite my love of traveling. However, if the occasion calls for it, I'll make an exception. I've found that attending panels is a great way to meet new people and broaden my professional network. I've met a portion of my closest companions on board, and it checks out. The best organizers work to put people who work well together on panels. If you can talk to each other for an hour on stage, you will probably want to spend more time getting to know each other.

CHAPTER 8
OVERCOMING CHALLENGES
There are many highs and lows in life. Every person has to deal with their unique set of challenges. You will be

able remain focus and composed under pressure if you learn how to overcome obstacles.

People have different and unique approaches towards overcoming challenges However, when things get tough, there are a few useful hints and techniques to follow. Choose one from the list that follows!

• Make a Plan

Despite the fact that you cannot predict the future, you can always prepare. Look at some of the instances from your daily life to discover what struggles you have faced. Make a plan to achieve the desired outcomes after evaluating them.

Assuming you work some place and can expect the sorts of difficulties you might confront, then, at that point, you can prepare. The same is true for schoolchildren. You can, for instance, learn and prepare for calendar management if time management is a problem.

•Don't forget that you are not alone

Everyone in the world has low points. Some individuals might handle or even conceal it better than others. Be that as it may, in all actuality, anything you are going through, there are other people who have had to deal with it as well. You won't be alone. Make an effort to connect with your network and community. In every setting of your life, share your emotions and concerns.

• Ask for Assistance

Always remember you are not alone, so you can get assistance. You shouldn't be ashamed of seeking for help. There are people who want to see you succeed, whether you choose to rely on a friend, a stranger, a mentor, or a loved one.

• Feel Your Feelings

You can't get over your emotions if you hide them. Instead, when feelings are ignored, they can stifle energy and even have negative effects on health. Set aside some margin to feel what you feel. This could come as contemplation. Alternately, writing can be a therapeutic and cathartic experience if you would rather record your feelings.

You may also be able to see your situation in a new light when you feel and share your feelings. You might discover novel solutions and overcome any obstacle as a result of this exercise.

• Accept Assistance

Getting assistance is only one side of the coin. On the other hand, you need to be open and ready to receive support. The people who help you actually care about you. When you need help, be willing to get it.

• Help Others

According to a well-known proverb, "What you give is what you get." Help out if you've been through something similar or if you have some advice for someone you know who is going through a difficult time! Being of assistance to other people can not only make them happier, but it can also make you happier.

•Think Big

When you're afraid of failing or even of making a decision, it can be easy to think small. Yet, to get extraordinary things done throughout everyday life, you must be available to facing challenges. With anything difficulties might emerge, consistently think and think beyond practical boundaries. You will accomplish more than you could have ever imagined in this manner. Try to keep your ideas from impeding your development.

• A positive mental attitude

Your thoughts become your actions. Learn to think positively with your mind. This will require some investment and practice. The first step is mental awareness. You can rehearse mindfulness through care procedures and reflection. Negative thoughts can be stopped in their tracks if you become proficient at acknowledging them and letting them pass.

thoughts can be stopped in their tracks if you become proficient at acknowledging them and letting them pass.

• Don't Give Up

When a challenge comes up, whether it's a big school test or an upcoming race, don't give up! Industriousness is an immense key to defeating difficulties. If you give up, you will not be able to overcome the obstacle or gain knowledge from it. Make a plan to overcome obstacles, feel your emotions, and ask for help when you need it.

• Work Smartly,

Not Hardly There are typically multiple approaches to completing a task. However, there is always only one best or optimal method. To work more intelligent as opposed to more enthusiastically, begin by working in reverse. Frame and characterize your objective. Making a plan for how to get there is the next plan. Conduct research to learn from the experiences of those who have gone before you. Make an assessment of your own skills and consider any room for improvement.

It takes time, perseverance, and a positive attitude to learn how to deal with difficulties. Regardless of your life circumstance, the tough situations will occur. However, with the right attitude and practice, you will always be able to overcome them and grow as a result!

CHAPTER 9
LEAVING A LASTING LEGACY

Entrepreneurs start their own businesses for a variety of reasons, including to fulfill a dream, find workarounds for unfulfilling careers, or increase their income. The desire to leave a legacy through their work motivates the majority of entrepreneurs. What does it mean to leave a legacy exactly? This is how Benjamin Franklin put it: Write something worth reading or do something worth writing if you want to avoid being forgotten when you die. Doing something that is worthy of writing about and changing the world is what it means to leave a legacy through your work.

It takes on a much deeper meaning when you consider your career as a way to leave a legacy rather than merely as a means of earning money. You want to make a lasting impression on a business when you put in your time, effort, and passion. You begin to wonder, "What is legacy?" How might I construct one?" Your legacy as a philanthropist is incomparably greater than an inheritance. Because it opens the door to genuine happiness in your life, learning how to leave a legacy is also a gift you give to yourself.

Many business owners are aware that they want their work to have an impact, but they are unsure of how to get there. You must first respond to a crucial question in order to truly leave a lasting impression: What's the significance here to leave a heritage? You don't want answers that are the same for everyone; what you want to leave behind as a legacy must be meaningful to you and unique. Learn how to leave a lasting legacy that will be remembered long after you have closed your business by following these steps.

•Have a sense of Direction

If you don't know what your life's purpose is, finding out how to leave a legacy can seem difficult and out of reach. Any action you take feels unfocused if you lack a sense of direction. Start with the end in mind when determining your purpose. In the end, you want your values to be remembered, so start by writing them down. Do you want your hard work to be remembered? Vision? Altruism? By recording your fundamental beliefs, you're ready to pinpoint what will make you generally satisfied - your motivation throughout everyday life - and afterward assemble your inheritance around it.

• Show off your natural abilities and skills.

Consider your heroes: the people who give you hope, encouragement, and inspiration. All things considered, as well as treating you with pride and regard, your legends additionally stand apart for particular abilities and gifts. Observing someone else's gift come to life is profoundly moving.

• Unlock Your Passion

 Living your passions brings you happiness in your life. Self-actualization is the process of utilizing the talents that come naturally to you and make you who you are.

Additionally, if you are content, you can only give to others. Consequently when you inquire "what's the point here?" It is to fulfill a global need. The key to leaving a legacy is to identify your passion and connect it to your purpose as well as your inherent abilities and skills. You are now prepared to put into action practical strategies for leaving a legacy at work once you have completed the work necessary to identify your true passions.

•Decide Your X Element

You can't leave a heritage on the off chance that you don't offer more benefit than any other person. You must capitalize on your X factor, or what sets you apart from others. Think about ways to make your product or service better so that people will remember it. For this to happen, your product needs to win over the hearts of your ideal customers by adding real value to their lives, so that no rival can come even close.

•Create A Business Map
Building a business that will continue to operate after you are gone is part of leaving a legacy. Creating something that can exist without you is more important than having a job to show up to every day. A mastermind business plan for achieving record profits is required to accomplish that.

•Inspire The Next Generation The key to happiness in life is having a fulfilling career. If you know how to leave investors a lasting legacy, you can also build a business that attracts future investment. However, leaving a legacy requires not only finding contentment for oneself but also inspiring others to do great things. This can be accomplished in a variety of ways, including cultivating a vibrant organizational culture and being an outstanding leader. It could mean helping others to refine organization processes, train new ability or oversee business funds. The employees you mentored, the leaders you inspired, and the lives you influenced will carry your legacy into the future.

•Offer in return
In the event that your qualities incorporate offering in return, schooling or monetary development, you should seriously mull over making an authority program or charitable establishment. A creative strategy for raising your brand and leaving a legacy is to develop a bespoke program that is compatible with your product. Giving back is another tried-and-true way to feel fulfilled: Commitment is one of the Six Human

Requirements that drive us throughout everyday life.

CONCLUSION

Right now, there are numerous opportunities! In fact, any time is a great time to take advantage of any opportunity that brings you closer to your goals. Many successful entrepreneurs share this conviction that regardless of the circumstances, you must move on and never give up! It is extremely easy to surrender to disappointment, however it is undeniably challenging to persevere through violent times and continue to push ahead. Entrepreneurship is never easy; There are as many as possible jumps. A business visionary crosses the seven degrees of agony starting with the beginning of a thought and proceeding with the whole way to the apex of their prosperity! However, the true business visionary is a tenacious worker who is resilient in rain, hail, or shine. He or she ought to get up and let go of the thoughts that he or she has an unshakeable faith in and a strong desire to see manifest.

You totally own your fantasy about beginning a business or making something remarkable. Only you can have faith in what you want to happen. Nonetheless, your vision may always be covered under the pad on the off chance that your fantasies are broken whenever. One cynical question that frequently crosses your mind is "is the concept sound enough to merit careful consideration?. And even if you are confident that the idea can be implemented, your mind will still ask, "Will it work? What is my limit?" Most people give up everything they have worked for in the present suspicion that we shouldn't make it happen! Remember that successful business people are excellent thinkers, but they rarely give their thoughts or ideas much thought. To see their ideas succeed, they take chances, put their minds to the test, and work toward their objectives. You will always be unable to foresee how they will show up, how forceful they will be, or how rapidly they will evaporate. Ideas can come to you in small drops or as a storm that wreaks havoc on everything it encounters. Nonetheless, similarly as downpour is a gift for individuals on The planet, thoughts are likewise a gift for the people who handle them. As a result, anyone who has an idea and knows how to put it into action has the potential to become an entrepreneur. Undertaking is a pitiful journey. Despite the fact that you totally own your idea, you want assets to transform it into a fruitful business. Developing generosity and associations with your inside and outer stakeholders is presently totally fundamental. When starting a business, organization plays a crucial role, and maintaining relationships with other business people can be helpful in times of difficulty.

Always remember to spend time with your loved ones because they are the ones who encourage you to trust your instincts, provide you with unwavering

support, and guide you through the most trying times.
"Continue to advance by placing one foot in front of the other!" is the mantra.